KRISTALLNACHT

STEPHANIE FITZGERALD

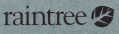

raintree

a Capstone company — publishers for children

Raintree is an imprint of Capstone Global Library Limited, a company incorporated in England and Wales having its registered office at 264 Banbury Road, Oxford, OX2 7DY – Registered company number: 6695582

www.raintree.co.uk
myorders@raintree.co.uk

Editorial Credits
Sarah Bennett, Jaclyn Jaycox, Angela Kaelberer, Kelli Lageson, Kathy McColley and Catherine Neitge
Originated by Capstone Global Library Limited
Printed and bound in China.

ISBN 978 1 4747 4320 4
21 20 19 18 17
10 9 8 7 6 5 4 3 2 1

British Library Cataloguing in Publication Data
A full catalogue record for this book is available from the British Library.

Acknowledgements
Alamy: John Frost Newspapers, 12, 84, Martin Shields, 52, 101 (left); Getty Images: Bettmann, 61, 88, Corbis Historical/Hulton-Deutsch Collection, 45, Galerie Bilderwelt, 76, Hulton Archive/Keystone, 63, Hulton Archive/Picture Post/Gerti Deutsch, 80, Keystone, 59, 71; Granger, NYC - All rights reserved: 11; Library of Congress, 19, 51; National Archives and Records Administration, 14, 41; National Archives/Press Association, 103 (top right); National Archives/ U.S. Army, 17; Newscom: akg-images, 22, 48, 65, 93, 96, akg-images/Bildarchiv Pisarek, 2, 46, 73, 83, 102 (left), EPA/STR, 6, 101 (right), Everett Collection, 28, Jewish Chronicle Heritage Images, 42, Picture History, 26, Pictures from History, 8, 56, 87, cover, St. Petersburg Times PSG/JOSEF FRIEDRICH COEPPICUS, 79, World History Archive, 95, ZB/picture alliance/ Agentur Voller Ernst, 98; Shutterstock: Everett Historical, 20, 25, 30, 33, 35, 38, 54, 66, 90, 102 (right), ilolab, throughout (background), Roman Nerud, 37, 100, U.S. Army/US Army Military History Institute, 103 (bottom left), XNR Productions, 47, 81

Every effort has been made to contact copyright holders of material reproduced in this book. Any omissions will be rectified in subsequent printings if notice is given to the publisher.

CONTENTS

On the morning of 10 November 1938, Jewish shop owners cleaned up what was left of their businesses. Storm troopers destroyed the windows of nearly 8,000 Jewish shops during what became known as the Night of Broken Glass.

CHAPTER ONE

NIGHT OF DESTRUCTION

Crash! Thirteen-year-old Arnold Fleischmann woke up with a start very early in the morning of 10 November 1938. Arnold lived in the town of Bayreuth, Germany, but he was staying with the Bloom family in the nearby city of Nuremberg while he studied for his bar mitzvah. This important religious ceremony for a Jewish boy was to take place on 12 November.

Arnold remembers German soldiers in brown shirts walking into his bedroom carrying daggers. "We pretended to be asleep even though they turned the lights on. They didn't bother us. They walked back out. They smashed all the kitchen dishes and china [cupboards], turned over the furniture and made sure just about everything was broken."

SA storm troopers stood guard outside a shattered Jewish-owned business in Vienna, Austria.

Arnold didn't know it then, but he was in the middle of a huge pogrom – an attack on Jewish people – that was going on in Germany and Austria. Known as Kristallnacht, the Night of Broken Glass, the pogrom was meant to frighten Jews into leaving their home countries. Chancellor Adolf Hitler and the National Socialist German Workers' Party, known as the Nazi Party, had controlled Germany since 1933. Hitler and the Nazis falsely blamed German Jews for many of the country's problems and had been making life in the country difficult for them since taking power. Beginning on the night of 9 November, Nazi leaders encouraged their private army, known as the Sturmabteilungen (SA), to destroy Jewish businesses, homes and synagogues. The streets and pavements were covered with shattered window glass. The SA storm troopers, and others, beat and even killed Jewish men.

After smashing up nearly everything of value in the house, the soldiers at the Bloom residence found several Torahs, which are religious scrolls. After setting fire to them, they arrested Mr Bloom and took him away. Arnold knew he had to find out what was happening to his own family in Bayreuth. He walked to a public telephone to call home. He learned that his father, grandfather and uncle had all been arrested earlier that morning.

THE NIGHT OF BROKEN GLASS

Kristallnacht is German for "night of crystal" and is often called the Night of Broken Glass. It got its name from the shattered glass that lined the streets after Jewish homes, businesses and synagogues were attacked. At the time, Germany didn't manufacture enough plate glass for its country's windows. It imported glass from other countries. It took a Belgian company six months to replace all the broken windows.

Arnold boarded a train and reached his home in Bayreuth at around 9.00 a.m. His grandfather and uncle were quickly released, but his father, a leader of the town's Jewish community, was being held in prison. Arnold was able to take some food to his father at the prison. About a week later, his father was released.

Arnold's planned bar mitzvah never happened. SA troops had burned Jewish synagogues and schools during Kristallnacht. "There was this total collapse of what it was like to be a Jew in Germany," he said. "After Kristallnacht I was afraid. I had seen enough of the cruelty of the Nazis and the so-called innocent bystanders who had seen these things and done nothing."

Arnold was right. During Kristallnacht, police officers and firefighters stood by while the SA and others destroyed and burned Jewish property, only making an effort to keep the flames from spreading to non-Jewish areas. Some townspeople threw rocks through shop windows, while others hurried past the violence with their faces turned away. A few brave people warned their Jewish neighbours or even hid them in

Firefighters worked to prevent fires from spreading to nearby homes, but did nothing to save a synagogue from burning in the aftermath of Kristallnacht.

their homes. But they weren't in the majority. As British news reporter Hugh Carleton Green observed, "Racial hatred and hysteria seemed to have taken complete hold of otherwise decent people. I saw fashionably dressed women clapping their hands and screaming with glee,

ND MORNING POST, FRIDAY, NOVEMBER 11, 1938 — 17

SYNAGOGUE FIRED IN BERLIN RIOTS

A telegraphed picture of the synagogue in Prinzregentenstrasse during the fire started by anti-Jewish rioters yesterday.

GERMAN MOBS' VENGEANCE ON JEWS

NATION-WIDE POGROM FOLLOWS DEATH OF DIPLOMAT

POLICE LOOK ON AT LOOTING AND LYNCHING

DR. GOEBBELS DESCRIBES OUTRAGES AS "JUSTIFIED INDIGNATION"

The entire Jewish population of Germany was subjected yesterday to a reign of terror, which began in the early hours of the morning and continued until late last night.

The pogrom, organised in revenge for the murder in Paris of the German diplomat, Herr vom Rath, by a young Polish Jew, started simultaneously all over Germany. No attempt was made by the police to restrain the savagery of the mobs.

Almost every synagogue in the country was burnt to the ground; scarcely a Jewish shop escaped being wrecked; looting occurred on a great scale, and parts of the fashionable shopping centre of Berlin were reduced to a shambles.

Jews of all ages and both sexes were beaten in the streets and in their homes, two were shot dead, numbers were lynched, and the caretaker of a synagogue is believed to have been burnt to death with his family. In Vienna there are understood to have been more than 20 suicides.

The outrages were described by Dr. Goebbels, Propaganda Minister, as "the justified and comprehensible indignation of the German people at the cowardly assassination of a German diplomat."

SIMULTANEOUS ATTACKS

ORGY OF DESTRUCTION

FROM OUR OWN CORRESPONDENT

BERLIN, Thursday Night.

An officially countenanced pogrom of unparalleled brutality and ferocity swept Germany to-day. Beginning in the early hours of this morning and continuing far into to-night, it puts the final seal to the outlawry of German Jewry.

Mob law ruled in Berlin throughout this afternoon and evening and hordes of hooligans indulged in an orgy of destruction. I have seen several anti-Jewish outbreaks in Germany during the last five years, but [illegible] **to have taken complete hold of otherwise decent people. I saw fashionably dressed women clapping their hands and screaming with glee, while respectable middle-class mothers held up their babies to see the "fun."**

Women who remonstrated with children who were running away with toys from a wrecked Jewish shop were spat on and attacked by the mob.

The fashionable shopping centre of the capital has been reduced to a shambles, with the streets littered with the wreckage of sacked Jewish shops and offices. No attempt was made by the police to restrain the rioters.

JEWS SHOT DEAD

The attacks on Jews and their property started all over Germany, as if by a concerted signal, soon after midnight, when the beer halls closed. In the course of the night two Jews were shot dead by armed mobs, one of them being an inmate of a camp for training Jewish emigrants at Bomsdorf.

The caretaker of the synagogue in the Prinz Regentenstrasse is reported [illegible]

MANY SUICIDES IN VIENNA

OLD MEN KICKED BY RIOTERS

FROM OUR OWN CORRESPONDENT

VIENNA, Thursday.

A torrent of misery and humiliation burst on the wretched Jewish population of Vienna at dawn to-day, when reprisals for the Paris murder began.

Search for concealed arms was the pretext under which thousands of Jewish homes were entered at daybreak and the occupants, men, women and children, were in many cases taken to the police station followed by shouting mobs.

In the course of the day not fewer than 15,000 Jews were searched for arms or documents. Several thousands were eventually allowed to go to their homes again, but many thousands more were taken from the police stations in tourist omnibuses and police vans to prisons or concentration camps.

SYNAGOGUE GUARDED

The attacks on synagogues began at about nine o'clock. The central [illegible] Cathedral of St. Stephen [illegible] by about 100 S.S. men, who wore steel helmets. This synagogue contains many records and catalogues of names, the loss of which would cause immense inconvenience to the authorities.

The main door had been burst in and considerable damage done inside the building before the guard was set; but it was the only one of the 21 synagogues and 71 Jewish prayer-houses of Vienna which was not set on fire.

Lads with tins of petrol accompanied the mobs, which attacked all the other synagogues. To every one of them the fire brigade was summoned, and fire engines remained near them all day.

Unspeakable panic gripped all the Jews in Vienna. About 50 are said to have attempted to commit suicide, and 21 are said to have succeeded.

GIRL PROTECTS FATHER

All cafés were raided and everyone present compelled to show his or her identity papers. I saw old men being chivvied along the streets by howling mobs, pushed down and kicked until they rose and ran again, staggering.

This was close to a great police station, before which 1,000 people were assembled. There was no policeman or [illegible]

KING & QUEEN TO CROSS OCEAN IN H.M.S. REPULSE

Navy's Big Part In Canadian Visit

TWO CRUISERS TO ACT AS ESCORT

Special Suites In Ships For Royal Party

By HECTOR C. BYWATER
"Daily Telegraph and Morning Post" Naval Correspondent

The King and Queen will make the voyage to and from Canada in the battle-cruiser Repulse.

In the announcement issued from Buckingham Palace last night it was stated that the Repulse would be escorted by two ships of the Second Cruiser Squadron.

It was in H.M.S. Repulse that the Duke of Windsor, then Prince of Wales, made his journeys to South America and South Africa in 1925.

The choice of the Repulse, one of our three remaining battle cruisers, is a happy one. She is, as I can testify from personal experience, having made many cruises in her, an excellent sea boat, though she is apt to be rather "wet" when travelling at speed in a sea-way.

SPACIOUS ACCOMODATION

As she has been employed before on royal cruises, the dockyard department knows exactly what structural alterations are necessary to equip her for this purpose. These, it is understood, are not of such a nature as seriously to impair the fighting efficiency of the ship.

As she was built to serve, when necessary, as a flagship, her accommodation is unusually spacious. The quarters designed for a flag officer and the immediate staff will presumably be reserved for the royal party, but additional cabins may be built for members of the suite, and, if precedent be followed, parts of the deck will be temporarily enclosed with recreation spaces, including a squash court.

The Repulse's commanding officer, according to the current Navy List, is Capt. J. H. Godfrey. She recently returned to England after more than two years' service in the Mediterranean [illegible]

TURKEY MOURNS KEMAL'S DEATH

NEW PRESIDENT TO BE ELECTED TO-DAY

FROM OUR OWN CORRESPONDENT

ISTANBUL, Thursday.

Istanbul, mourning the death of Kemal Ataturk, the creator of the Republic, is in semi-darkness to-night. All cinemas, theatres and night clubs are closed. In the restaurants there is no music.

But for official news bulletins, all broadcasting programmes have been cancelled. Since 9.5 a.m. to-day, when the flag on the President's Dolma Bagtche Palace was hoisted at half-mast, the nation has been plunged in gloom.

Kemal Ataturk was 58. For many months it had been known that he was suffering from cirrhosis of the liver. Three weeks ago he rallied, but on Tuesday it was realised that his death was imminent.

Abdul Halik Renda, President of the Kamutay, or Grand National Assembly, has assumed the interim Presidency of the Republic. He has convened Parliament for 11 a.m. to-morrow, when a new President will be elected.

It is almost certain that Gen. Ismet Ineunu, 58-year-old ex-Premier and Ataturk's staunch lieutenant throughout Turkey's war of independence, will be elected by a big majority.

NATION UNITED

The Turkish nation is obviously united in the desire that Ataturk's great work shall be continued along the path which he has marked out. In an official communiqué, issued to-day, the Government states:

"To-day we mourn the loss of Ataturk, who always put his confidence in the people. Thanks to this faith he achieved all his great objectives. The continuation of these works he has left to the nation, and the Turkish people will keep them alive eternally.

"The youth of Turkey will always defend the Republic which he has left as a precious legacy, and will always march in the paths he trod. Kemal Ataturk will live for ever in the history of Turkey and in the hearts of his countrymen."

On 11 November 1938, *The Daily Telegraph* reported on the attacks on Jewish properties across Germany.

while respectable middle-class mothers held up their babies to see the 'fun'."

During Kristallnacht, nearly 8,000 Jewish-owned businesses and homes were damaged and looted. Hundreds of synagogues were destroyed, most by fire, and nearly 100 Jews were killed. Another 30,000 were sent to concentration camps. News of the huge pogrom was printed in newspapers throughout Europe and the United States. But little or no effort was made to help the Austrian and German Jews.

Kristallnacht sent a message to the world that the Nazis wanted the Jews out of Germany and its territories, and would do whatever they needed to accomplish that goal. The lack of reaction from the rest of the world also sent a message to the Nazis. Kristallnacht was just the beginning.

More than 65 million soldiers from 30 countries fought in World War I.

CHAPTER TWO

GERMANY IN RUINS

How did something as violent as Kristallnacht happen? Its roots can be traced to the anger and despair the German people felt following World War I.

World War I began on 28 June 1914, when a Serbian man, Gavrilo Princip, assassinated Austrian Archduke Franz Ferdinand and his wife as they travelled in a car through Sarajevo. Princip and other Serbians were angry about Austria-Hungary's control of Bosnia and Herzegovina. On 28 July Austria-Hungary declared war on Serbia. Russia came to Serbia's defence, and on 1 August Germany declared war on Russia. By the end of August 1914, Britain, France, Belgium and Japan were involved in the fighting. Germany, Austria-Hungary, the Ottoman Empire and Bulgaria formed an alliance called the Central Powers. Their opponents were the Allied Powers of Britain, Russia and France, along with several other countries. In 1917 the United States also joined the Allies.

By the time it ended on 11 November 1918, World War I was one of the bloodiest and most expensive wars ever, with nearly 9 million soldiers and 13 million civilians killed and more than 20 million people seriously wounded. The war cost the countries involved £143 billion. The Allied nations shouldered the biggest burden, about £97 billion.

After the war, the Allies blamed Germany for starting the war. The Allies wanted to make sure that Germany would never be able to start another war. As part of the Treaty of Versailles, which was signed on 28 June 1919, Germany lost much of its territory in Europe. They also were told to pay reparations of £25 billion to the Allied countries for the money they spent fighting the war. Germany was left in ruins and its people were furious. They blamed not only the Allies for their situation.

The signing of the Treaty of Versailles brought World War I to an end.

Many Germans also blamed their Jewish neighbours.
Many people in Germany and other European countries
were anti-Semitic. They hated Jews and wanted to
blame them for their problems. These Germans thought

A STAB IN THE BACK

When Germany surrendered in November 1918, many Germans called this "forced" surrender the *Dolchstoss*, meaning "stab in the back". Many believed that German Jews had forced the surrender. But that wasn't true. German army leaders asked the government to seek terms of surrender because the soldiers weren't able to continue fighting. But German military leaders and certain politicians deliberately hid this information from the German people. They claimed that German Jews and members of various socialist and liberal political parties had pressured the government to surrender. They referred to them as the "November criminals".

that the German Jews had betrayed German soldiers by pushing the government to surrender and sign the Treaty of Versailles.

Anger over the outcome of the war led to new political parties, such as the Nazi Party, which formed in 1919 as the German Workers' Party. Adolf Hitler, who had served as a corporal in the German army during World War I, joined the party soon after it formed. By 1921 Hitler was leading the party, which was known as the National Socialist German Workers' Party.

Despair over the conditions of the Treaty of Versailles wasn't the only factor that helped the Nazis gain power in Germany. During the 1920s Germany experienced a period of major inflation. Prices for goods rose to extremely high amounts as the German currency, the mark, became worth very little. "My father was a lawyer," remembers Walter Levy, a German-born consultant, "and he had taken out an insurance policy in 1903, and every month he had made the payments faithfully. It was a 20-year policy, and when he cashed it in it was only enough for a single loaf of bread." Prices increased rapidly. For example, a person would order a cup of coffee costing 5,000 marks at a cafe. By the time the waiter brought the bill, the price had increased to 7,000 marks.

German marks became so worthless, people burned the paper money as fuel to heat their homes and cook their meals.

People used their nearly worthless cash to buy things they didn't want or need and then bartered for what they did need.

As life in Germany became more desperate, Hitler's popularity grew. Many Germans liked Hitler's promises to not only restore Germany's world position but also to

raise the country to new heights of power. He pledged to revive the economy, rebuild the army and regain the territories that Germany lost after World War I, as well as expand into new ones. Hitler believed that the Germans and other Europeans of Nordic descent formed a "master race" that was superior to all other ethnic groups. He

referred to these people as Aryans – ideally, people with fair skin, blonde hair and blue eyes. He believed Aryans were responsible for all the advances in world history, and that Germany would become great again only if the country rid itself of non-Aryans, especially Jews. He also wanted to expel all other ethnic minorities and people who were physically or mentally disabled. How exactly he planned to do this wasn't known to many people at the time – perhaps not even to

An enthusiastic crowd saluted Adolf Hitler as he went by in a parade.

JEWS IN GERMANY

About 500,000 Jews lived in Germany in 1933. About one-fifth of them weren't German citizens. They were immigrants from Eastern Europe, mainly Poland. Whether they were citizens or not, most Jews were loyal members of German society. Many were poor, but there was also a strong Jewish middle class. Many Jewish people owned or worked in small businesses, such as clothing or furniture shops, or were doctors and lawyers.

Hitler's bitter anti-Semitism was the keystone of his plan for Germany. He believed that Jewish people held too much power and were responsible for almost everything bad that happened in the world. Though Hitler's ideas must have made them uncomfortable, few Jewish Germans realized until too late the depth of his hatred for Jewish people, or the lengths to which he would go to force them out of Germany.

A Jewish bookshop in 1920s Berlin

Hitler himself. But as the Nazi Party grew in power and strength, that all changed. Soon Hitler's plans for non-Aryan people were terrifyingly clear.

Hitler was determined to isolate and harass the Jews in Germany to the point where they would want to leave the country. At this time in history, the Nazis were not focused on the mass murder of Jews – they wanted to make Germany *Judenfrei*, meaning "Jew free", or *Judenrein*, meaning "pure of Jews".

A FATEFUL ANNIVERSARY

Kristallnacht occurred on the 15th anniversary of a failed Nazi attempt to take over the government, called the Beer Hall Putsch. Adolf Hitler and about 20 other Nazis walked into a Munich beer hall on 8 November 1923, where a political meeting was taking place. Gustav von Kahr, the state commissioner general of Bavaria, led the meeting. Hitler fired a gun at the ceiling and called for a new national government, which he would lead. The crowd cheered him, but after Hitler left the hall, Kahr alerted the military to be on the lookout for the Nazis.

The next morning Hitler found out that his coup hadn't worked out the way he had planned. But he decided to make a final stand. At 11.00 a.m. Hitler and about 2,000 Nazis marched to the centre of Munich. During a stand-off with police, someone fired a shot, which killed a police sergeant. The police opened fire on the demonstrators. Four policemen and sixteen Nazis were killed, and many others were wounded.

Hitler fled and hid at a friend's home for two days before he was found and arrested. He was sentenced to five years in prison. While in prison, Hitler wrote the first volume of *Mein Kampf* (*My Struggle*), which told of his anti-Semitic beliefs

A crowd gathered to hear a speaker at the Beer Hall Putsch in Munich.

and outlined his goals for Germany. Hitler was released on parole on 20 December 1924, after only nine months in jail. Two months later he again was leading the Nazi Party. But he had no intention of making the mistake of an attempted coup again. Hitler was determined to be elected Germany's leader, which would allow him to legally implement his plans to restore Germany to its former glory.

Huge crowds greeted Adolf Hitler, who would rapidly rise to power in Germany's government.

CHAPTER THREE

HITLER'S RISE TO POWER

After Adolf Hitler's release from prison in 1924, the Nazi Party began to rebuild. Hitler's strength as an orator, combined with Germans' frustration over the crumbling national economy, helped persuade more people to support the party. But the Nazis didn't have much election success until 1930, when they received 18 per cent of the total vote. With that victory, the Nazis went from the smallest party in Germany to the second largest.

In July 1932 Nazi candidates were elected to 230 of the 608 seats in the German Parliament, the Reichstag. The Reichstag was dissolved in September, and new elections were held in November. In the 1932 election, the Nazis lost some of their seats. Hitler ran for president, but lost to incumbent president Paul von Hindenburg. The following January, though, Hindenburg appointed Hitler to the position of chancellor, which was the head of the democratic government.

President Paul von Hindenburg (centre) appointed Adolf Hitler as chancellor in the hope that doing so would keep the Nazi Party under control.

The next month the Reichstag building was set on fire, and the Nazis blamed members of the Communist Party, who opposed the Nazis. Hitler used the incident to seize even more power from Hindenburg. On 23 March, members of the Reichstag passed the Enabling Act, which effectively ended democratic government in Germany and gave Hitler absolute power.

Hitler wasted no time exercising his new powers. On 1 April 1933, the Nazis organized a nationwide boycott of Jewish-owned businesses. Lists of Jewish shops were distributed in every town. The Jewish symbol, the Star of David, was painted on Jewish-owned shopfronts, as were Nazi

PRESIDENT VS CHANCELLOR

After World War I, the president was the head of the German government. Paul von Hindenburg held the elected position from 1925 until 1934. Under the German constitution, the president had the power to appoint the chancellor, who reported to both the president and the Reichstag. Today, though, the power of the positions is reversed. The office of president is largely a ceremonial position. The German chancellor is the head of the government, running the country with the aid of parliament.

A Nazi storm trooper stood in front a Jewish store in Berlin, Germany, beside a sign reading "Germans, defend yourselves, do not buy from Jews."

swastikas and the word Jude, the German word for Jew. Anti-Jewish graffiti also appeared on the shopfronts. People were encouraged to report any Germans who ignored the boycott, and SA troops stood outside Jewish businesses to threaten anyone who tried to enter.

But the boycott wasn't a success. Most Germans didn't support it, and some even went out of their way to visit Jewish-owned businesses. The government cancelled the boycott after the first day. But later that month, Hitler outlawed non-Aryans from working in government jobs. In parts of Germany, kosher butchering, the Jewish way of preparing animals for

KOSHER BUTCHERING

Orthodox Jews strictly follow the laws of the Jewish holy book, the Torah. They adhere to traditional practices, which include eating only foods that are kosher. Hitler's law against kosher butchering made them face some difficult choices.

Schlomo Wahrmann's father, a kosher butcher, ignored the law and kept providing kosher meat for the Jews of Leipzig. Wahrmann later wrote about this experience:

"Often, my younger sister would carry the [koshering knife] to the chicken market because we were confident the Gestapo [secret police] would not apprehend such a young girl. Nonetheless, my mother remained tense."

Other Orthodox Jews chose to live without meat. Jewish newspapers in Germany printed vegetarian recipes and, in 1935, Germany's League of Jewish Women published a vegetarian cookbook.

slaughter, was also made illegal. Another law limited the number of non-Aryan students allowed to attend public schools and universities, allegedly to reduce crowded classes.

President Hindenburg died on 2 August 1934. With Hindenburg gone, Hitler had no limits on his quest for power. He combined the positions of president and chancellor and named himself führer – the absolute ruler of Germany. The democratic constitution was no longer in effect. Immediately, Hitler went after his political enemies. Storm troopers arrested and imprisoned or killed hundreds of people whom Hitler believed threatened his leadership.

Hitler continued to work towards a Germany that was Judenfrei. "Jews Not Wanted" signs started to appear in hotels, theatres, sports stadiums and restaurants. Similar signs were posted on the roads leading into villages and towns.

The Reichstag passed the Nuremberg Laws on 15 September 1935. They defined Jews not as people who followed the Jewish religion but as those who had

Signs reading "Jews Not Wanted" were posted all around Germany.

Jewish ancestry, such as three Jewish grandparents. The laws stripped German Jews of their citizenship and forbade them from marrying non-Jewish Germans or flying the German flag. Life was difficult for German Jews, and by 1938 many had emigrated to countries elsewhere in Europe or to the United States. Some who wanted to leave were unable to, either because of cost or quotas. But many stayed, believing that German citizens would soon come to their senses and oust Hitler from power. For many of them, it was an error in judgement that would prove fatal.

NIGHT OF THE LONG KNIVES

Sometimes even Hitler's friends weren't safe from his anger and paranoia. He became convinced that the SA was planning to seize his power. On the night of 30 June 1934, Hitler ordered the executions of his old friend, and head of the SA, Ernst Röhm, and several of Röhm's officers. The purge became known as the Night of the Long Knives, from a German saying about revenge.

A FRIGHTENING SYMBOL

Symbols became an important part of the Nazi persecution of Jewish people. Hitler selected the swastika to represent the Nazi Party in 1920. The name of the hooked cross comes from the Sanskrit word *svastika*, meaning "good fortune" or "well-being". For ancient people it may have represented the sun moving through the sky. It's still used as a sacred symbol by religions such as Buddhism and Hinduism. Hitler may have first seen the symbol as a child when he attended a school in a monastery in Lambach, Austria. The swastika was on the Nazi flag and also decorated military uniforms and vehicles.

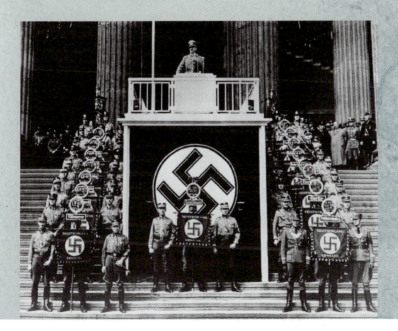

WHO WAS ADOLF HITLER?

Although Adolf Hitler became a world leader, his early life was marked by failure. Hitler was born 20 April 1889, in Braunau am Inn, Austria, to Alois and Klara Hitler. Alois had two older children from an earlier marriage. When Adolf was four years old, his brother Edmund was born, followed by sister Paula two years later. Edmund died of the measles when Adolf was 10.

Adolf did well in primary school, but struggled once he entered secondary school. He loved to draw and wanted to attend an art school. His father wanted him to work in a government job and sent him instead to a technical school. Adolf hated it and spent much of his time misbehaving and playing pranks. One teacher said that Adolf "reacted with ill-concealed hostility to advice or reproof; at the same time, he demanded of his fellow pupils their unqualified subservience, fancying himself in the role of leader." Alois Hitler died when his son was 13 and wasn't around to prevent Adolf from leaving school at the age of 16.

After leaving school, Hitler spent his time reading, drawing, painting and visiting art galleries and museums. In October 1907, at age of 18, he applied to the Vienna Academy of Fine Arts. When he was rejected, it was a huge blow to him, as was his mother's death two months later. Soon after, he returned to Vienna and again applied to the

Academy of Fine Arts. Again, he was rejected. He ran out of money but didn't try very hard to find a job. By the winter of 1909, he was living in a homeless shelter. He did odd jobs and also found some work as an artist, selling postcard-sized paintings. He still read extensively, focusing on politics, philosophy and German history. The books he read helped to form the ideas he later put into practice as head of the Nazi Party and Germany.

Hitler moved to Munich in 1913, volunteering for the German army when World War I began in 1914. He was wounded in action and received five medals, but only rose to the rank of corporal – the second-lowest rank in the army. After the war, Hitler remained in the army and worked as an undercover agent.

In September 1919 he received an assignment to investigate the new German Workers' political party. He was impressed with the party's ideas, which were similar to his own. He joined the party, which would later become the Nazi Party. Before long he was giving fiery speeches about Germany's problems and how to solve them. Hundreds of people came to party meetings just to listen to him. In 1921 he became the party's leader – a position he would keep for the rest of his life.

Thousands of German soldiers participated in the annual Nuremberg Rally. The rallies of the Nazi Party showcased Germany's military power to the rest of the world.

CHAPTER FOUR

THOUSAND-YEAR REICH

The official name for the Nazi government was the Third Reich. Reich means "empire" in German. Germans used the term to refer to periods in their country's history. During the First Reich, Germany was part of the Holy Roman Empire, from about 962 until 1806. The Second Reich was the German Empire, which began in 1871 with the unification of Germany and lasted until the collapse of the country in 1918 after World War I. Hitler referred to the Third Reich as the Thousand-Year Reich because he predicted the Nazis would rule Germany for 1,000 years.

Breaking the rules of the Treaty of Versailles, Hitler formed a new army, navy and air force. German soldiers moved into the Rhineland, an area in western Germany

near the borders of Belgium, Luxembourg and France,
on 7 March 1936. According to the Treaty of Versailles,
the area was to be demilitarized. No German military
forces were permitted to be stationed in the Rhineland.
But no countries tried to stop them. These
countries were still recovering from World
War I. Rather than confront Hitler, British
and French leaders tried to work with him.
They thought that if they gave Hitler what
he wanted, he would be content and stop
demanding more. But the opposite was
true. The more he got away with, the more
confident Hitler became. He decided that
Austria was next on the list for a
German takeover.

Hitler met with Austrian chancellor
Kurt von Schuschnigg in February 1938 and
demanded more power for the Nazi Party
in Austria. Schuschnigg refused and was
eventually forced to resign by members of
the party. Arthur Seyss-Inquart, the leader of

the Austrian Nazi Party, took over. Seyss-Inquart invited the German army to invade Austria, which it did on 12 March. The result was the Anschluss, a union between Germany and Austria.

Enthusiastic Austrians welcomed the German takeover in March 1938.

About 200,000 Jewish people were living in Austria at the time. This was nearly equal to the total number of Jews who had been forced to emigrate from Germany in the early 1930s. On 11 March, knowing the Germans would soon occupy their country, Austrian Nazis in Vienna staged an attack on their Jewish neighbours.

Any Jewish person caught on the streets was beaten or humiliated. Some were forced to clean army toilets or

Jewish people were forced to clean the streets of Vienna after the Anschluss. Onlookers stood by while Jews were made to perform the tasks.

scrub slogans supporting former chancellor Schuschnigg off the pavements. Jewish businesses were looted and destroyed, and Jewish people were arrested or fired from their jobs. The Austrian police did nothing to stop the Nazi attackers. In many cases, they merely stood by and watched.

DISCRIMINATION AGAINST JEWISH PEOPLE

Discriminatory laws and policies weren't the only things that made life hard for Jewish people in Germany. The rude treatment they received from their non-Jewish neighbours also made day-to-day life difficult.

In public, some Germans would point out people they thought were Jewish by commenting on their looks or an imagined smell. But they often were mistaken.

Historian Marion Kaplan wrote about one such incident: "In one case, a woman remarked upon three children seated across from her in a train compartment. She admired the two 'Aryan' types and denigrated [belittled] the darker girl. The father of the two finally told her that the two blondes had a Jewish mother and the darker one was 'Aryan'."

The Austrians' actions against the Jewish people impressed the German Nazis. The *Schwarze Korps*, a weekly Nazi newspaper, reported: "They have managed to do overnight what we have failed to do up to this day in the slow-moving, ponderous north. In Austria, a boycott of the Jews does not need organizing – the people themselves have instituted it with honest joy."

CZECHOSLOVAKIA'S FATE

In September 1938 Czechoslovakia became a victim of Europe's hopes to keep Hitler happy. Hitler wanted the Sudetenland to be under German control. This region, with its large German population, had become part of Czechoslovakia after World War I. When the leaders of Germany, Britain, France and Italy met in Munich to discuss the situation, the head of Czechoslovakia was not invited. At the meeting, the leaders signed an agreement that transferred the Sudetenland to Germany. When Czechoslovakian President Eduard Beneš protested the decision, he was told by Great Britain's leadership that they were not willing to go to war with Germany over the Sudetenland.

The graffiti on Jewish shops in Austria warned the owners that if they cleaned off the hateful slogans, they would be sent to a concentration camp.

A number of Jewish Austrians saw no way out and committed suicide. A report in *The New York Times* said that as many as 170 Jewish people were taking their own lives every day. Thousands more left Austria for neighbouring countries, some travelling as far as Britain and the United States.

JEWISH EMIGRATION

Between 1933 and 1939, about 95,000 German and Austrian Jews legally emigrated to the United States. Approximately another 60,000 Jews settled in Palestine in the Middle East, which at the time was ruled by Britain as part of the peace agreement made after World War I. In the 1920s many Jewish people had emigrated to the area to create a Jewish state. In the late 1930s, German Jews saw Palestine as the perfect place for them to escape the Nazis' tyranny.

Thousands of Jewish people left Nazi Germany after the Nuremberg Race Laws of 1935. The laws took away German citizenship rights from Jews, making them "subjects of the state".

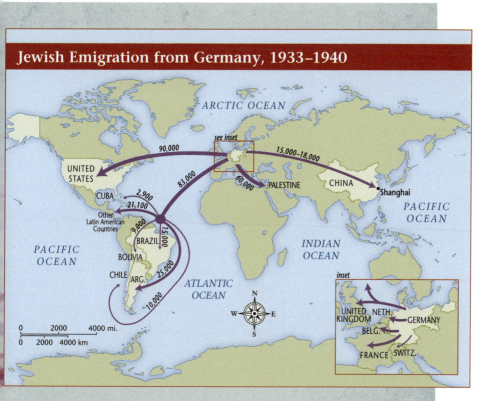

Jewish Emigration from Germany, 1933–1940

In Palestine, they believed they would truly be welcomed. But it was the British government, not the Jewish people living there, who decided which people would be allowed into Palestine. The British government set severe limits on the region's immigrant quotas.

As fewer European nations agreed to accept Jewish refugees, thousands of German, Austrian and Polish Jews travelled to Shanghai, China. The city was one of the few places in the world that had no visa requirements.

But all countries had quotas limiting the number of immigrants they would allow to enter their borders. Countries such as the United States made their immigration policies as difficult as possible for Jewish refugees. Officials would demand documents they knew would be impossible for the

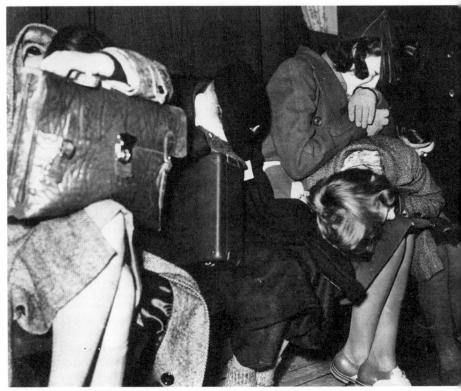

The first Kindertransport arrived in Harwich, England, on 2 December 1938, carrying nearly 200 Jewish children. The British government agreed to let children from Germany enter the country and stay temporarily until the "crisis was over".

A FAILED ATTEMPT AT HELP

US President Franklin D. Roosevelt was concerned about what was happening to the Jews in Austria and Germany. In March 1938 he invited representatives from around the world to a conference in Evian-les-Bains, France. He asked them to form a committee to help political refugees emigrate from Austria and Germany.

The Evian Conference took place in July. Representatives from 32 countries attended. Although Roosevelt had called for the conference, he didn't attend or send a high-ranking government official. Instead, he sent a friend, businessman Myron Taylor.

Of all the countries gathered at the conference, only the Dominican Republic offered to increase its immigration quotas. Other countries, including the United States and Britain, lowered their quotas. As in Germany, many people around the world were anti-Semitic.

The United States was also in the middle of the Great Depression. American politicians and citizens were afraid that unemployed Jewish immigrants would compete with Americans for the few jobs available. The failure of the Evian Conference encouraged Hitler to keep persecuting the Jews. He realized that although other countries condemned what he was doing, they weren't willing to step in to stop him.

immigrants to get or would simply reject their applications. This frustrated Nazi leaders in Germany, who had planned to make life so difficult for Jewish people that they would choose to emigrate to other countries. But no other country was willing to take so many of them.

Nazi leaders realized they had to take more drastic action against the Jewish population. In a series of new laws and decrees, the government increased its efforts to identify and isolate its Jewish residents. On 26 April 1938, Hermann Göring, the Nazi economic minister, said that all Jewish holdings valued at more than 5,000 reichsmarks (approximately £925) would have to be registered. This rule allowed the Nazis to keep track of, and use, Jewish wealth in Germany.

Beginning in June 1938, more than 2,000 Jewish and other people were arrested on charges of "race pollution". Simply living among the Aryan population was considered a crime. The people who were arrested were taken to one of the four concentration camps in Germany – Dachau, Buchenwald, Lichtenburg or Sachsenhausen.

A FAMOUS IMMIGRANT

The Nazis' desire to rid themselves of all Jewish people robbed them of some of the most brilliant minds of the time. Among those was the noted physicist Albert Einstein.

Einstein was born in 1879 to a Jewish family in Ulm, Germany. As a young man, he developed the mass/energy equivalence formula, E=mc2. His theory of general relativity, published in 1916, helped people to understand how space, time, light and gravity work together. He won the Nobel Prize for physics in 1921.

By 1933 Einstein was alarmed by the rise of the Nazi Party in Germany. He renounced his German citizenship and moved to the United States, saying, "I shall live in a land where political freedom, tolerance and equality of all citizens reign." He settled in New Jersey and became a US citizen in 1940. He continued his scientific research and discoveries until his death in 1955.

A policy took effect in August 1938 requiring Jewish men with names not recognized as Jewish to use the middle name "Israel" and women to use the middle name "Sarah". According to both the Hebrew and Christian Bibles, Israel and Sarah were ancestors of the Jews. The names would allow the Nazis to easily identify anyone having Jewish ancestry. In October, Jewish passports were no longer valid. New passports were stamped with the letter "J" and Jews were forced to carry special identity cards.

A Jewish passport from 1939 Nazi Germany was stamped with a large "J" on the left side to identify the holder, Max Reinhold, as Jewish.

At a meeting on 14 October 1938, Göring gave the signal that new, drastic measures were about to begin. "The Reich must eradicate doubtful elements from the population," he told his colleagues. "Namely, the last remaining Jews."

The Nazis just needed the right opportunity. Less than a month later, that opportunity came to them through the actions of a 17-year-old Polish Jew who had grown up in Germany. His name was Herschel Grynszpan.

A WORLDWIDE DEPRESSION

The Great Depression of the 1930s was unique – it was an economic downturn that affected the whole world rather than just one country. Nations tried to boost their own industries by attaching high tariffs to foreign goods. But the policy to tax imports slowed foreign trade, which made the Depression drag on for years. It is estimated that 30 million people worldwide were without jobs by 1932. In countries such as Germany, Italy and Japan, the instability was a leading cause of the rise of fascism – a government system with extreme right-wing views.

CONCENTRATION CAMPS

Early concentration camps were built as detention and work camps for political prisoners, people whom the Nazis considered enemies and people who broke the laws of the Reich.

The first such camp opened in the town of Dachau in southern Germany in 1933. The Sachsenhausen camp opened in 1936, followed by Buchenwald in 1937. Although individual prisoners

were often murdered, these camps were not death camps designed for mass extermination of prisoners. The Nazis' six killing centres, Auschwitz-Birkenau, Belzec, Chelmno, Majdanek, Sobibor and Treblinka, were built later.

In the concentration camps, the inmates worked for 14 to 16 hours a day, often breaking and hauling stones for building projects. They were forced to stand in a line in the hot sun, sometimes for 15 hours at a time. During this time the prisoners didn't receive any food or water, and they couldn't move to use the toilet. At Buchenwald and Sachsenhausen, the prisoners worked to enlarge the camps. At Dachau, they were forced to sew the Star of David on thousands of striped uniforms for prisoners to wear.

Two prisoners at Buchenwald concentration camp supported a fellow prisoner, because fainting was often an excuse to kill inmates who could no longer work.

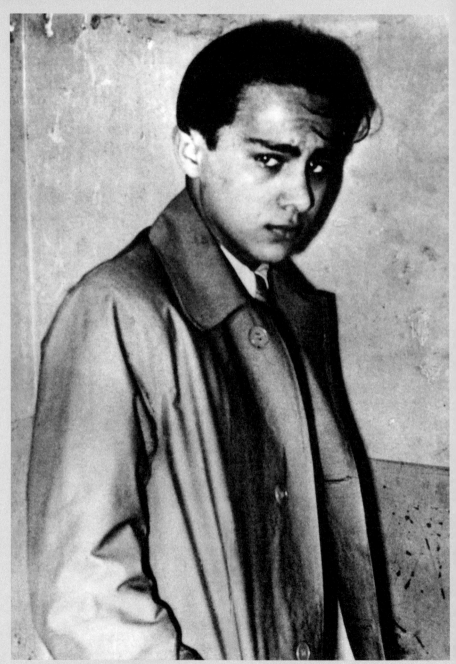
Herschel Grynszpan wanted to avenge brutal Nazi oppression.

CHAPTER FIVE

A SHOOTING IN PARIS

Herschel Grynszpan was born in 1921 in Germany. His parents, Zindel and Rivka, were Jews who had emigrated from Poland 10 years before Herschel was born. He attended a yeshiva – Jewish school – in Frankfurt as a teenager. At the age of 15 he left the yeshiva and returned to his parents' home. He wanted to emigrate to Palestine, but wasn't allowed to do so because of his age.

Herschel's parents were concerned about what was happening to Jews in Germany and wanted their son to be safe. They sent him to live with his uncle and aunt, Abraham and Chawa Grynszpan, in Paris, France. Herschel, who had a Polish passport, was allowed to travel to Belgium to visit another uncle. From there, he crossed into France illegally in September 1936.

Because he was in France illegally, Herschel wasn't able to work or attend school. He spent his days in the cafes and cinemas in Paris. His Polish passport had expired in January 1938, and French authorities informed him in August that he had to leave the country. Afraid to return to Germany, he stayed illegally in France, under constant fear of being discovered. He kept up with what was happening to the Jews in Germany by reading the *Pariser Haint*, a Yiddish-language newspaper published in Paris.

Herschel was alarmed to read a story on 31 October 1938, reporting that 12,000 Polish Jews had been deported from Germany in the last few days of October. On 3 November he received a postcard from his sister, Berta. As Herschel read the postcard, his worst fears were realized. His sister wrote: "You undoubtedly heard of our great misfortune. I will describe to you what happened. On Thursday evening rumours circulated that all Polish Jews had been expelled from a city. But we didn't believe it. On Thursday evening at 9 o'clock a Sipo [security policeman] came to us and informed us that we had to go to Police Headquarters. Almost our

Thousands of Polish Jews were expelled from Germany, but Polish authorities refused to take them. They lived in Zbaszyn on the Polish-German border for many weeks in a refugee camp.

entire quarter was already there. A police van brought
all of us right away to the Rusthaus. All were brought
there. We were not told what it was all about, but we saw
that everything was finished for us. Each of us had an
extradition order pressed into his hand, and one had to
leave Germany before the 29th. They didn't permit us to
return home anymore. I asked to be allowed to go home
to get at least a few things. I went, accompanied by a
Sipo, and packed the necessary clothes in a suitcase. And
that is all I saved. We don't have a pfennig [penny]. More
next time."

A few days later, Herschel received another postcard
from his sister. The family had been taken by train to the
village of Zbaszyn, near Poland's border with Germany.
They were stuck there while the Polish government
decided if they could take the refugees. Berta wrote, "We
are very poorly fed. We sleep on straw sacks. We have
received blankets. But, believe me . . . we won't be able
to stand this much longer." She closed the message by
begging her brother to send money.

Jews deported from Germany cooked in buckets outside their living quarters in
Zbaszyn, Poland, where they lived in stables.

On 6 November Herschel asked his uncle Abraham
for money to send to his family. Abraham refused, saying
he had little money to spare and even if he did, there
was no address to send it to. Herschel was angry at his
answer, and the two got into a shouting match. Finally,
Abraham told Herschel that if he didn't like living under
his rules, he could leave. Furious, Herschel stormed out
of the apartment with the little money he had. Before he
left, though, Abraham threw 200 francs at him. Instead
of attempting to send the money to his family, Herschel
came up with a different idea about how to spend it. He

used a little of the money to buy food and rent a room at a small hotel, where he spent the night. By that time, Abraham had calmed down and went out to look for his nephew. He never found him.

At 8.35 a.m. the next morning, Monday 7 November, Herschel walked into *A La Fine Lame* (At the Sharp Blade), a shop that sold guns and ammunition, just as it was opening. "I want to buy a revolver," he told the owner.

Herschel paid 210 francs for a 6.35 mm revolver and another 35 francs for a box of ammunition. The owner, Monsieur Carpe, showed him how to load and fire the gun. Herschel was supposed to fill out a declaration form for his gun and hand it in to the police. He never made it to the police station, though. Instead he went to a cafe. In the cafe's bathroom, he unwrapped the gun and loaded five cartridges in its chambers. He then walked out of the cafe and down the street.

By 9.30 a.m., Herschel had reached his destination – the German Embassy. He politely asked to see the German ambassador and was told he was not in. At that same moment, a man walked past Herschel on his way

out of the embassy. It was the
ambassador, Count Johannes
von Welczeck. He had heard
Herschel ask for him but
didn't want to delay his
morning walk, so he didn't
stop. That decision probably
saved his life.

Once inside the embassy,
Herschel told porter Henri
Nagorka that he had an
important document and

German diplomat Ernst vom Rath

needed to see someone who knew German secrets.
Nagorka offered to take the document, but Herschel
insisted that he needed to deliver it personally. Nagorka
then took Herschel to see Ernst vom Rath, the only
official who was on duty that early in the morning.
Vom Rath told Herschel to sit down, but Herschel
remained standing.

When vom Rath asked to see Herschel's document,
the young man reached into the inside pocket of his

jacket and pulled out his gun. "You are a *sale boche* [French for a "dirty Kraut"] and in the name of 12,000 persecuted Jews, here is the document!" he screamed.

Herschel fired five shots at vom Rath at point-blank range, hitting him twice. But to Herschel's surprise, the diplomat didn't fall dead to the ground. Vom Rath staggered to his feet as he called for help. Herschel stood there, staring at his victim. He made no attempt to reload the gun and shoot vom Rath again.

Nagorka ran to the room after he heard the shots and vom Rath's calls for help. More help arrived as a doctor and a French police officer called Autret were called to the scene. Instead of trying to escape, Herschel just sat passively in a chair.

On the way to the police station, Herschel spoke to Autret. "I've just shot a man in his office," he said. "I do not regret it. I did it to avenge my parents, who are living in misery in Germany."

As soon as Hitler learned of the shooting, he ordered his personal physician to Paris to take care of vom Rath.

A FINAL MESSAGE

At the hotel where Herschel Grynszpan spent the night before the shooting, he wrote a note to Abraham and Chawa Grynszpan on the back of a postcard with a photo of himself that he kept in his wallet. He started the note in Hebrew with the words "with God's help". Then he continued in German: "My dear relatives, I couldn't do otherwise. God must forgive me. My heart bleeds when I think of our tragedy and that of the 12,000 Jews. I have to protest in such a way that the whole world hears my protest, and this I intend to do. I beg your forgiveness."

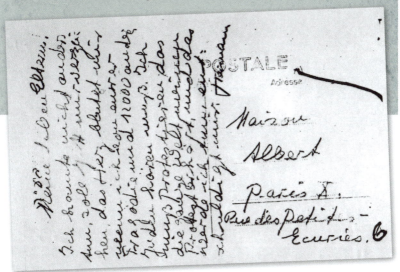

A handwritten postcard by Grynszpan to his aunt and uncle indirectly hinted at the shooting to come.

The Nazis sponsored an elaborate funeral of Ernst vom Rath, who was assassinated by Herschel Grynszpan.

CHAPTER SIX

NIGHT OF TERROR

News of the assassination attempt was first reported on 8 November, just as members of the Nazi Party were gathering in Munich to commemorate the anniversary of the Beer Hall Putsch. Joseph Goebbels fired up the crowd by speaking about Herschel Grynszpan's attack.

The assassination gave the Nazis the excuse they needed to stage a widespread assault on Jewish people in Germany and Austria. Nazi leaders later claimed that Germans were outraged about vom Rath's shooting and took it out on the country's Jewish people. But this story was just Nazi propaganda. Nazi leaders at the highest level ordered the pogroms that took place on 9 November and the following day.

The Nazi propaganda ministry ordered all of Germany's newspaper editors to make sure the story of the assassination dominated the front page of every paper. An article headlined "The Criminals" in the Nazi newspaper *Völkischer Beobachter* read: "It is clear that the German people will draw their own conclusion from this new deed. It is an impossible situation that within our frontiers hundreds of thousands of Jews should control our shopping streets, places of entertainment and as 'foreign' landlords pocket the money of German tenants, while their racial comrades outside call for war against Germany and shoot down German officials."

Hitler learned about Ernst vom Rath's death in an afternoon phone call but pretended to learn about it as he ate dinner in Munich's old town hall chamber that night. In a "drama carefully

NO VOICE

While the Nazi newspapers expressed outrage over the assassination and called for revenge, German Jews remained publicly silent. All Jewish newspapers and magazines were banned, and the Jewish community had no voice to comment on the event.

staged by Hitler and Goebbels," witnesses recalled
that after he received a telegram, Hitler pushed away
his plate and spoke "agitatedly" to Goebbels, who
was sitting next to him. Goebbels later said that they
discussed demonstrations against Jews that had recently
taken place around Germany. He said Hitler told him
that although the party should not organize similar
demonstrations, it should not stop any that might occur
"spontaneously". Other people who were there said they
heard Hitler say that "the SA should be allowed to have
a fling".

Hitler then got up and left the hall. This was
unusual. Hitler usually gave the closing speech at these
gatherings. But this was all part of Hitler's and Goebbels'
plan. Now no matter what was said or happened after he
left, Hitler could always claim that he had never given
any specific orders. Instead, Goebbels gave the closing
remarks, saying, in part: "I have news for you here
tonight, to demonstrate what happens to a good German
when he drops his guard for one moment. Ernst vom
Rath was a good German, a loyal servant of the Reich,

working for the good of our people in our embassy in Paris. Shall I tell you what happened to him? He was shot down! In the course of his duty, he went, unarmed and unsuspecting, to speak to a visitor at the embassy, and had two bullets pumped into him. He is now dead. Do I need to tell you the race of the dirty swine who perpetrated this foul deed? A Jew! Tonight he lies in jail in Paris, claiming that he acted on his own, that he had no instigators of this awful deed behind him. But we know better, don't we? Comrades, we cannot allow this attack by international Jewry to go unchallenged. . . I ask you to listen to me, and together we must plan what is to be our answer to Jewish murder and the threat of international Jewry to our glorious German Reich!"

After hearing Goebbels' speech, Nazi leaders believed that Herschel Grynszpan wasn't the only one who was to blame for vom Rath's death; it was all Jews – and they all needed to be punished. A message went out from the headquarters of the German secret police, the Gestapo, to all local police bureaus, alerting them that the SA would be carrying out demonstrations against

Joseph Goebbels was a high-ranking Nazi and close friend of Hitler, who named him minister of public enlightenment and propaganda.

Jews that night. The police were told not to interfere, except to prevent looting. They were also told to expect the arrests of 20,000 to 30,000 Jews, particularly those who were wealthy. Police were also told that although synagogues and community centres could be burned to the ground, businesses and homes were to remain intact. The Nazis wanted the Jews out, but they wanted to save their property so the Nazis could confiscate it after the Jewish owners were forced out.

By midnight on 9 November, attacks on Jewish businesses, homes and synagogues were well underway in the Third Reich. Mobs roamed the streets of German cities and towns, shouting anti-Semitic slogans.

In Munich, mobs torched the first synagogue at midnight. Firefighters tried to control the flames as they began to spread to a nearby Jewish school. But the SA officers cut their hoses and added petrol to the fire. The firefighters had no choice but to watch both buildings burn.

In Berlin the pogrom didn't start until 2.00 a.m. on 10 November, to give police time to get ready. Police identified Jewish property that would be destroyed and set up roadblocks to keep traffic away from those

A synagogue in Berlin was just one of many synagogues destroyed during Kristallnacht.

areas. They also wanted firefighters standing by to make sure that fires didn't spread from synagogues to nearby homes or businesses. By dawn, nine of the city's twelve synagogues had been burned.

In Cologne the police handed out axes and weapons to the SA and other members of the crowd. They also supplied a list of names and addresses of Jewish property to be destroyed. The police didn't want to risk any Aryan property accidentally being targeted. Seventeen Jewish shops in the city centre were destroyed.

In Nuremberg, the SA destroyed nearly all Jewish property before turning on the Jews themselves. Nine Jewish people were murdered. Some were beaten to death, one was thrown from the window of his house, and another was thrown down his own staircase repeatedly until he died. Ten more Jewish people were reported to have committed suicide.

If Jewish-owned property was left in Nuremberg after Kristallnacht, the Nazis stole it. Many Jewish people were forced to sign over their properties for a fraction of what they were worth. A synagogue worth more than 100,000 reichsmarks (£18,000) was sold for 100 reichsmarks (£18). Nazi officials told Jews that they must agree to sell or they would be killed. By

14 November most of the Jewish property in Nuremberg was in the hands of the local Nazi Party.

THOSE WHO DARED SPEAK OUT

Some non-Jewish Germans had the courage to speak out against the Nazi violence during Kristallnacht. Pastor Julius Von Jan led a Lutheran congregation in the town of Oberlenningen in the Swabia region of Germany. The Sunday after Kristallnacht, he preached to his congregation about the evils of the pogrom: "Houses of worship have been burned down with impunity [without fear of punishment]. Men who served our nation and have done their duty have been thrown into concentration camps because they belong to a different race. Our nation's infamy is bound to bring about divine punishment."

Von Jan was quickly punished for his words. A Nazi mob beat him and threw him onto the roof of a shed. They then destroyed his house. Von Jan was arrested and tried. He served five months of a sixteen-month prison sentence. In 1943 he was drafted into the army. After surviving the war, he returned to his church. He died in 1964.

The attacks were especially violent in Austria and
the Sudetenland, perhaps because SA members there
were eager to show their loyalty to Germany. Freddie
Knoller, who was a boy in Vienna, Austria, at the time,
later recalled the terror that gripped him and his family

Jewish women in Austria were forced to sit in public with cardboard signs stating,
"I have been excluded from the national community".

that night: "Somewhere around 11 that night, we heard a noise in our courtyard, and looking down we saw the storm troopers talking to our caretaker. He took them into the building. My mother became quite hysterical: 'What are they going to do? Where are they going? Are they coming up to us?' My father turned off the lights so that the apartment was in darkness. Suddenly we heard a woman's shrill voice, a screaming voice, and we heard the glass of a window breaking. We heard a thud in the courtyard. We looked down and saw a body lying there. We didn't know who it was until the woman, Mrs Epstein from the first floor, came running into the courtyard, screaming and going to her husband's body."

As the looting and destruction wound down on 10 November, the arrests began. Jewish men of all ages were rounded up and marched through the streets as their German neighbours shouted insults at them.

Fourteen-year-old Esther Ascher went out into the streets of her hometown of Breslau that morning. She remembers, "The streets were deserted except for SS men, marching with a Jewish male between them."

Esther walked through the streets and saw destruction of property everywhere. Soon she had seen enough and turned around to go home. "The picture was the same: SS men leading Jews who followed them as innocent lambs. . . . From that point on life changed for me. I had but one goal, to leave Germany."

During the week following Kristallnacht, more than 30,000 Jewish men were arrested and sent to the concentration camps at Buchenwald, Dachau and Sachsenhausen. The arrests marked a change in Nazi policy. Before Kristallnacht, Jewish people had to have committed some type of offence against the Reich to be sent to the camps. The men arrested and sent to the camps after Kristallnacht were guilty of only one thing. They were Jewish.

The Nazis didn't plan to keep the Jewish people arrested after Kristallnacht in the camps very long. Their imprisonment was intended to encourage them to leave

Germany. The prisoners were told that they would
be released if they were ready to leave the country
immediately. Gestapo officials also warned the prisoners
that if they told anyone about what happened at the
camps, they would immediately be arrested and
returned to them.

Nazi storm troopers led Jewish men from the town of Baden-Baden,
Germany, to be transported to the Dachau concentration camp in 1938.

THE KINDERTRANSPORT

After Kristallnacht, the British Committee for the Jews of Germany appealed to members of Parliament to allow German immigrants into the country. After much debate, it was decided that an unspecified number of children younger than 17 would be allowed into Britain. The programme was known as the Kindertransport. The first transport left Germany less than one month after Kristallnacht. About 10,000 children made the journey. The last transport left Germany on 1 September 1939. The last transport left the Netherlands on 14 May 1940, when that nation surrendered to Germany. In Britain, some children were sent to orphanages or group homes, some were taken in by foster families, and others worked on farms. Most of the children never saw their families again.

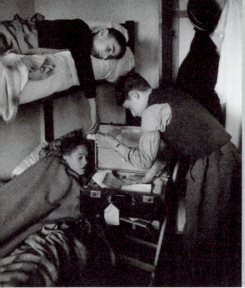

Refugee children stayed at a holiday camp at Dovercourt Bay near Harwich after arriving in Britain in December 1938. The children were part of the Kindertransport operation.

Kristallnacht, 9–10 November 1938

- • Cities where synagogues were destroyed
- Former borders, 1933
- Land added to Germany, 1938

As a result of the Kristallnacht pogrom on the night of 9 November and the following day, nearly 8,000 Jewish-owned shops, warehouses and homes were damaged or destroyed. Nearly 300 synagogues were burned or otherwise demolished. As many as 2,500 Jews – including men, women and children of all ages – died as a result of Kristallnacht, mostly in concentration camps.

SANCTIONS AGAINST JEWS

The emboldened Nazis published new decrees against Jews on 14 November 1938. Jews could no longer attend concerts, films and other public performances. The next day, German Education Minister Bernhard Rust issued an order that banned all Jewish children from German schools. "After the ruthless murder in Paris, no German teacher can any longer be asked to give lessons to Jewish schoolchildren," he said. "It goes without saying that it is intolerable for German pupils to sit in the same classroom with Jews." Jewish children were allowed to attend only schools run by the Jewish communities.

On 3 December the Decree on the Utilization of Jewish Property forced all Jewish businesses to be sold to non-Jews, usually for prices far below their market value. Starting on 6 December, Jewish people were forbidden to walk or drive in certain places. In Berlin the ban covered all public recreational facilities, including theatres, concert halls, museums, parks and swimming pools. Any Jewish person caught in one of the banned places could be fined 150 reichsmarks (£28) or spend six weeks in prison.

Jewish people were also forbidden to walk on many of the streets in Berlin. Jewish people who

Jewish schools were closed in 1942 as part of the extermination plan for European Jews.

lived on the banned streets were told to leave and find somewhere else to live. Hotel owners asked for a decree that would ban Jews from their hotels. Soon other cities and towns enacted similar restrictions.

SUNDAY EXPRESS November 13, 1938

Sunday Express

Founded by LORD BEAVERBROOK

No. 1,037 — LONDON, NOVEMBER 13, 1938 — TWOPENCE

LATE EXTRA

THE POGROM GOES ON

German Jews fined £83,000,000; Forced to pay for riot damage; Banned from business; Barred from all social life

GERMANY'S Jews last night suffered the most smashing blows of all.

By decree, signed by Field-Marshal Goering, they were forbidden from January 1 to own, or manage, any shop, factory, mail-order house or any other kind of business.

ALL SUCH BUSINESSES WHICH THEY NOW OWN WILL BE TAKEN FROM THEM, IF THEY HAVE FAILED TO GET RID OF THEM BEFORE JANUARY 1, AND HANDED OVER TO ARYANS.

They are also forbidden to pursue any "handicraft" and no Jew may be a foreman or chief clerk in any factory, store, or business. They must not, in fact, hold any responsible post at all.

Further, under the same merciless decree, Jews must immediately, at their own cost, repair all damage to their property caused during the last three days by the Nazi rioters.

All insurance money claimed by them will be confiscated by the State, and as a monetary compensation for the assassination in Paris of Herr vom Rath the whole Jewish community of Germany has been ordered to pay a collective fine of £83,000,000—a thousand million marks.

This sum will be appropriated by the State in order to fill its empty coffers.

In their social life the Jews must also suffer decrees as drastic as those that threaten their economic existence.

All Jewish newspapers are prohibited. Jewish schools are closed.

DR. GOEBBELS, BY DECREE YESTERDAY, FORBIDS ALL JEWS FROM ATTENDING ANY CONCERTS, CINEMAS, THEATRES, VARIETY HALLS, LECTURES, DANCES OR PUBLIC EXHIBITIONS.

In Berlin an exhibition of "the eternal Jew" has opened in the burnt-out Reichstag building. This exhibition pillories the Jewish race in placards and pictures and is drawing large crowds.

Persons who admit them to such entertainments are warned that they will suffer "severe penalties."

An official warning has been issued that further decrees regulating Jewish economic life will be forthcoming. It is assumed that this means the restoration of the Ghetto of the Middle Ages, and close control of the income and spending of all Jews.

Already there is scarcely an hotel or restaurant left which Jews are permitted to enter. Over the doors or in the windows all over Germany are placards "Jews forbidden."

No matter how tolerant the owner or manager may be it makes no difference. He must turn Jews away. He dare not refuse.

I know several of these tolerant restaurant managers and owners, writes a correspondent from Berlin, but they shrug their shoulders and say, "These are our orders. We cannot disobey."

Some of them tell me that they are sorry they have had to tell those Jews who have been "guests" in their restaurants for twenty years or more that they can no longer come in.

Tolerant Germans were yesterday looking aghast at the wrecked Jewish shops and discussing the new anti-Jewish measures. They fear that these measures will be a serious hindrance to the efforts of the Western democracies in building up an understanding with Germany.

The Jews themselves are in terror.

THOUSANDS HAVE ALREADY BEEN ARRESTED ALL OVER GERMANY AND TAKEN TO HASTILY IMPROVISED CONCENTRATION CAMPS, WHERE THEY WILL UNDOUBTEDLY ENDURE GREAT AND PERHAPS FATAL HARDSHIPS.

IN THEIR FEAR THOUSANDS OF JEWS IN BERLIN HAVE LEFT THEIR HOMES AND ARE AFRAID TO RETURN. THEY ARE WANDERING FROM PLACE TO PLACE VISITING FRIENDS, WHOM THEY ARE BEGGING FOR

(Continued On Page 17)

AN ILL WIND BLEW RICHES

HUNDREDS of men, women and children took part in a treasure hunt on Weymouth beach yesterday.

An easterly gale had disturbed the sands, revealing a rich harvest of coins and jewellery lost by summer visitors.

Errand boys even left their bicycles to join in the search, while scores of people went without their midday meal.

Hardly a square yard of the beach was left uncombed.

A few days ago Weymouth Corporation announced that the year's profit from the beach (deck chairs, kiosk sites, etc.) was nearly £6,000. This figure whetted the searchers' appetites.

THE AIRMAN BEAT THE ADMIRAL

IN UNIVERSITY POLL

All the nice girls may love a sailor, but St. Andrews, the Scots university town, prefers the air force.

This is how they voted for their new Lord Rector yesterday:—

Air Vice-Marshal Sir David Munro	416
Admiral of the Fleet Sir Roger Keyes	298
Majority	118

Sir David's supporters as they marched through the streets sang:—

"Any time down polling booth way,
"Any hour of Saturday,
"You've got to vote,
"Vote for Sir David Munro."

And as they sang, they danced the Lambeth Walk.

Supporters of the admiral found election songs and parodies easier to concoct.

"Keyes, Keyes, Lord of the Seas,
"The ideal Rector and Student Protector"

was one of their slogans.

PACT SIGNING DAY

In Rome diplomatic circles, says the Exchange, it is stated that the signing of the Anglo-Italian agreement by Lord Perth and Count Ciano, the Italian Foreign Minister, will take place on Wednesday.

Why We Can't Get The Planes

AT a time when a nation is striving with every ounce of its energy to build a great air force as swiftly as possible, this is an example of what is happening.

It was told to a Sunday Express representative by the chairman of a world-famous British motor-car firm—a firm renowned for precision engineering. He said:—

"My company erected one of the best-equipped aircraft engine factories in the country. We made an air engine which passed its Air Ministry type tests. Then I asked the Ministry for an order.

"Excuses"

"I received no order. Instead I was given all kinds of excuses—first that the engine would not fit available air frames. I altered the size. Then I was given other excuses.

"Eventually I was told that I could not have an order because I was not a member of the ring—that is, a firm on the approved list drawn up just after the last war.

"I kept on badgering. Eventually I was offered a sub-contract to make bits and pieces of an engine designed by one of the approved firms, but on the extraordinary condition that I signed an undertaking not to make air engines of a certain size for several years.

Factory Idle

"I refused to sign. Our factory, which had cost many thousands of pounds to erect and equip, stood idle. So did the trained engineers on our staff, among the finest in the country.

"And meanwhile the Air Force was crying out for engines. Orders were even being placed in America, but we could not have them because we were not in the ring.

"Recently large sub-contracting orders have been placed with us and we are now in full production, but we still cannot be given direct contracts. The claims of our own engine are still ignored. The monopoly is still unbroken.

"I intend to make a public statement on the matter at the annual meeting of my company."

Crisis-Strain Postponed This Bride's Wedding

A bride who collapsed on the eve of her wedding, fixed for October 15, when her father and her bridegroom were mobilised during the crisis, walked smiling happily under an arch of lifted swords at St. John's Church, Weymouth, yesterday.

She was Miss Mary Eileen Homan, daughter of Captain K. A. Homan, R.N., and Mrs. Homan, of Lockeen, Seaton, Devon.

The bridegroom was Lieutenant-Commander Mark Taylor Collier, of H.M.S. Alecto, submarine depot ship, Portland.

Arrangements for the wedding in October had to be cancelled at such short notice that many people turned up at the church.

Tooth Weighing Over Four Pounds Found

A mammoth tooth, seven inches long and weighing 4lbs. 3oz., has been found at Cleethorpes during excavations for a new hotel.

It was dug out of the glacial clay five feet below the surface.

—Weather—

MILD AGAIN

UNSETTLED, with occasional rain, is the weather outlook for today. But it will remain mild.

Strong south to south-west winds are expected, reaching gale force in exposed places.

The Man Who Started The War Meets The Man Who Ended It

You heard them in "In Town Tonight" last night—Sergeant E. D. Thomas, of Brighton, Sussex (left), who fired the first shot of the great war for Britain, and Mr. F. H. Pennington, of Hove, who sent out the original "Cease Fire" signal. Although they live in adjoining towns they had never met until approached by the B.B.C. for this broadcast.

Capone, Due For Release, May Become A Farmer

AL CAPONE, formerly America's No. 1 gangster, is due for release from Alcatraz Prison, off the Californian coast, early next year. He is serving a sentence for income-tax evasion.

But America is not frightened at the prospect of Capone's freedom, for he is a sick man, reported to be suffering from brain disease.

Even if his health were not broken, he could not get together his old gang, for they are either dead, or working on their own or in other gangsters' interests.

Capone, it is believed, is going to live on a farm near Hobart, Indiana, which was recently bought by an old confederate of his, Michael Corrozzo (Dago Mike).

It is said that £20,000 is being spent on the farm, in preparation for Capone's arrival.

The Little Man Has Saved £1,400,000,000

The little man, the small investor, has put £1,400,000,000 in the National Savings movement alone, said Mr. Walter Elliot, Minister of Health, speaking at the Bonar Law College, Ashridge, Herts, last night.

He also said that a married man of fifty-four, joining the Government's voluntary pension scheme this year, would, for payment of 1s. 3d. a week, get pension rights which would otherwise cost 15s. a week.

SILVER BAN

The German Government yesterday curtailed domestic consumption of silver for certain household utensils.

Goods for export are exempted from the restrictions.

BISHOP HONOURED

The Bishop of Gloucester (Dr. A. C. Headlam), who is chairman of the Church of England Council on Foreign Relations, has been appointed a commander (first class) of the Order of the White Rose of Finland.

SIR N. HENDERSON

Sir Nevile Henderson, the British Ambassador in Berlin, underwent a minor operation in London yesterday. His condition is satisfactory.

The Cuckoo In The Nest

When charged with stealing two railway tickets at Rathmore, Co. Kerry, yesterday, a man said:—

"I escaped from Wallasey Mental Home in Lancashire in April. I did not like the place because there were a lot of crazy people there and it was getting on my nerves."

not have an order because I was not a member of the ring—that is, a firm on the approved list drawn up just after the last war.

"I kept on badgering. Eventually I was offered a sub-contract to make bits and pieces of an engine designed by one of the approved firms, but on the extraordinary condition that I signed an undertaking not to make air engines of a certain size for several years.

Factory Idle

"I refused to sign. Our factory, which had cost many thousands of pounds to erect and equip, stood idle. So did the trained engineers on our staff, among the finest in the country.

"And meanwhile the Air Force was crying out for engines. Orders were even being placed in America, but we could not have them because we were not in the ring.

"Recently large sub-contracting orders have been placed with us and we are now in full production, but we still cannot be given direct contracts. The claims of our own engine are still ignored. The monopoly is still unbroken.

"I intend to make a public statement on the matter at the annual meeting of my company."

Crisis-Strain Postponed This Bride's Wedding

A bride who collapsed on the eve of her wedding, fixed for October 15, when her father and her bridegroom were mobilised during the crisis, walked smiling happily under an arch of lifted swords at St. John's Church, Weymouth, yesterday.

She was Miss Mary Eileen Homan, daughter of Captain K. A. Homan, R.N., and Mrs. Homan, of Lockeen, Seaton, Devon.

The bridegroom was Lieutenant-Commander Mark Taylor Collier, of H.M.S. Alecto, submarine depot ship, Portland.

Arrangements for the wedding in October had to be cancelled at such short notice that many people turned up at the church.

Tooth Weighing Over Four Pounds Found

A mammoth tooth, seven inches long and weighing 4lbs. 3oz., has been found at Cleethorpes during excavations for a new hotel.

It was dug out of the glacial clay five feet below the surface.

—Weather—

MILD AGAIN

UNSETTLED, with occasional rain, is the weather outlook for today. But it will remain mild.

Strong south to south-west winds are expected, reaching gale force in exposed places.

60 Members Of Family At Diamond Wedding Party

A DIAMOND WEDDING party at Brighton yesterday was attended by sixty members of one family. It was the first time in the history of the family that

LATEST NEWS
Telephone: Central 8000

RADIO - - - PAGE 8

all its members had gathered together.

They were the children, grandchildren and great-grandchildren of Mr. and Mrs. Williams Coney, of Ditchling-rise, Brighton. The party was held in the Royal Pavilion, former residence of George IV.

The party was organised by the Rev. J. A. Coney, a son, who brought his wife and two children from America.

Another member was a daughter

Capone, Due For Release, May Become A Farmer

AL CAPONE, formerly America's No. 1 gangster, is due for release from Alcatraz Prison, off the Californian coast, early next year. He is serving a sentence for income-tax evasion.

But America is not frightened at the prospect of Capone's freedom, for he is a sick man, reported to be suffering from brain disease.

Even if his health were not broken, he could not get together his old gang, for they are either dead, or working on their own or in other gangsters' interests.

Capone, it is believed, is going to live on a farm near Hobart, Indiana, which was recently bought by an old confederate of his, Michael Corrozzo (Dago Mike).

It is said that £20,000 is being spent on the farm, in preparation for Capone's arrival.

The Little Man Has Saved £1,400,000,000

The little man, the small investor, has put £1,400,000,000 in the National Savings movement alone, said Mr. Walter Elliot, Minister of Health, speaking at the Bonar Law College, Ashridge, Herts, last night.

He also said that a married man of fifty-four, joining the Government's voluntary pension scheme this year, would, for payment of 1s. 3d. a week, get pension rights which would otherwise cost 15s. a week.

SILVER BAN

The German Government yesterday curtailed domestic consumption of silver for certain household utensils.

Goods for export are exempted from the restrictions.

BISHOP HONOURED

The Bishop of Gloucester (Dr. A. C. Headlam), who is chairman of the Church of England Council on Foreign Relations, has been appointed a commander (first class) of the Order of the White Rose of Finland.

SIR N. HENDERSON

Sir Nevile Henderson, the British Ambassador in Berlin, underwent a minor operation in London yesterday. His condition is satisfactory.

A London newspaper reported on Germany's actions against its Jewish citizens.

CHAPTER SEVEN

AFTERMATH OF KRISTALLNACHT

Newspapers worldwide published stories about what happened in Germany and Austria on 9 and 10 November. People in other countries were horrified and demanded an explanation.

Adolf Hitler and Joseph Goebbels responded to the worldwide newspaper stories by holding a press conference for foreign correspondents in Berlin on 11 November. Goebbels told the journalists that German citizens were responsible for the violence because of their anger about Ernst vom Rath's assassination. But the journalists weren't satisfied with Goebbels' explanation. They pressured him to tell the truth.

For once, Goebbels appeared to be taken aback. He insisted that if Jews around the world continued to spread exaggerated stories about the event – as he claimed they were doing in US newspapers – "they would be digging the graves of the Jews in Germany."

The day after the press conference, Goebbels was back to business as usual. He believed that the Nazis had got away with Kristallnacht and was confident that no matter what they did to the Jews, there would be no consequences. The Nazis also hoped that being candid about their plans to get rid of the Jews would encourage other nations to find a place for Jewish refugees.

But despite the world's outrage over Kristallnacht, other European governments didn't condemn the Nazi government's actions. Many countries were unwilling to upset international trade, risk involvement in another war or create policy problems at home. British Prime Minister Neville Chamberlain still refused to speak out against Hitler, even though members of the press and the British Parliament pressured him to do so. In France, meanwhile, the subject was never brought up by the government.

Neville Chamberlain served as British prime minister from May 1937 to May 1940.

Even Jewish people living outside of Germany didn't have a strong response. Three days after Kristallnacht, representatives of the General Jewish Council met in New York City, USA, to discuss a response to the pogrom. According to a report in *The Jewish Week*, the members of the council were worried about anti-Semitism in the United States and decided "that there should be no parades, public demonstrations or protests by Jews".

Only one world leader publicly condemned the Nazi government and its actions – US President Franklin D. Roosevelt. On 15 November, he said, "The news of the last few days from Germany has deeply shocked public

Franklin D. Roosevelt was the first and only world leader to speak out against the Nazi government after Kristallnacht.

opinion in the United States. Such news from any part of the world would inevitably produce a similar profound reaction among American people in every part of the nation. I myself could scarcely believe that such things could occur in a twentieth-century civilization."

Roosevelt then brought the US ambassador home from Berlin – something that had not happened since World War I. But the situation for Jews in Germany didn't improve.

It's impossible to say whether anything – except another world war – could have made Hitler give up his plans for Germany. But perhaps if the rest of the world had acted sooner, the horrible things that happened to European Jews could have been avoided.

It took World War II for countries to band together to stop Hitler. The war began on 1 September 1939, when Germany invaded Poland. Britain and France declared war on Germany on 3 September. A year later Germany entered into an alliance with Italy and Japan, when leaders of the three nations signed the Tripartite Pact. The three countries, together with Bulgaria, Croatia,

Hungary, Romania, Slovakia and Yugoslavia, formed the Axis powers. The Soviet Union was also a German ally for a time, as Hitler and Soviet Premier Joseph Stalin had signed a non-aggression plan in August 1939.

German soldiers invaded Poland in September 1939. It was the beginning of World War II in Europe.

By June 1941 the Nazi empire covered most of Europe as the German army marched across the continent, meeting little resistance. Denmark, Norway, Belgium, the Netherlands, France and Luxembourg all fell under

German control. But Hitler then made a fatal error by invading his former ally, the Soviet Union, on 22 June 1941. In December 1941 the United States entered the war after Japan bombed the US naval base at Pearl Harbor, Hawaii. The United States joined Britain, the Soviet Union and China as the Allied forces.

At the same time that the Germans were expanding their empire, they were increasing the number of "undesirables" within that empire. Forcing Jewish people to emigrate or placing them in concentration camps no longer satisfied them. The Nazis came up with a new plan known as the Final Solution. The policy was coordinated at the highest levels of the Nazi Party and government at a conference in Wannsee, a suburb of Berlin. That solution was genocide – an attempt to wipe out the entire Jewish population. It would come to be known as the Holocaust.

After World War II began, the Nazis forced Jews to live in designated areas of a city, called ghettos. Jewish people lived in miserable conditions, isolated from the non-Jewish community. The Germans established more than 1,000 ghettos in Central and Eastern Europe. About 400,000 people were crowded into the Warsaw ghetto in Poland alone. Concentrating Jewish people in ghettos made it easier for the Nazis to round them up and send them to concentration camps.

In July 1944 Majdanek in Poland was the first death camp liberated by Soviet troops. Andrew Werth, a correspondent for *The Times of London* and the British Broadcasting Corporation (BBC), toured the camp one month after the liberation. His bosses at the BBC refused to air his report, though. The horrors that Werth reported were so shocking that they thought his story was based

A sign at one of the entrances to a ghetto in Lodz, Poland, warned: "Jewish area: entrance forbidden." Lodz became the second-largest ghetto created by the Nazis in Poland.

on Soviet propaganda. It was not until more camps were liberated that people began to understand and believe what had been happening.

THE DEATH CAMPS

When the Nazis invaded Poland in September 1939, they suddenly had millions more Jews in their control. Forcing Polish Jews and other people to emigrate wasn't going to work any better than it had in Germany. Instead, the Nazis decided to kill them.

The first wave of killings was carried out by special execution squads that followed the German army into Poland – as well as local people willing to cooperate with the Germans. The main targets were male Jews, Roman Catholic priests, Communists and members of the wealthy or intellectual classes.

The execution squads rounded up their victims, took them to the outskirts of town, and forced them to dig mass graves. Then they lined their victims up on the edge of the graves and mowed them down with machine guns. Before the end of the war, women and children would be among the victims of the execution squads.

As the Germans advanced on the Soviet Union, millions more Jews came under their control. Nazi leaders came up with a new execution method for the Jews. They were placed in vans designed to allow the vehicles' exhaust to blow into the vans. The people inside died of carbon monoxide poisoning within 15 minutes.

Before long, the Nazis realized that the methods of killing Jews were too slow. Hitler and his

Deported Jewish people arrived at Auschwitz death camp in Poland. Auschwitz-Birkenau was the largest of the German concentration and extermination camps. Over 1 million Jewish people are thought to have died there, most of them in the gas chambers.

advisers decided that all the Jews of Europe were to be murdered - the Final Solution. The Nazis came up with the plan in January 1942 to expand some of their concentration camps into extermination camps.

The Germans, and their allies in Europe, rounded up Jews anywhere they could find them and sent them to extermination camps, which were equipped with gas chambers. Other prisoners were shot, beaten to death or hanged. Thousands more died from the deadly infectious diseases, such as typhoid fever, malaria and tuberculosis, that swept through the camps. Still others starved to death. The Nazis murdered 6 million Jews: two-thirds of the Jews living in Europe in 1939.

Although most people did not know what was going on inside the camps, Allied leaders did. The only solution they could find to ending the genocide, though, was to defeat Germany as quickly as possible. They believed that winning the war was the only way to end the Holocaust.

A storeroom held the clothes of murdered prisoners.

The war in Europe ended in April 1945, but
Hitler never paid for his crimes. He shot himself on
30 April 1945, as the Soviet army advanced on his bunker
in Berlin. The next day, Goebbels and his wife poisoned
their six children before committing suicide. But the war
continued in the Pacific until after the Allies dropped
atomic bombs on the cities of Hiroshima and Nagasaki
in early August 1945. Japan agreed to surrender on
14 August, and the war formally ended in September
with an Allied victory.

Once again, Germany was brought to its knees after
a world war that it had largely caused. The country
split into two after the war ended. East Germany was
under the Soviet Union's control and had a communist
government, and West Germany was a democracy. East
and West Germany were united into one Germany on
3 October 1990. Today, the unified Germany is a
democracy and is a strong ally of Europe and the
United States.

PUNISHING WAR CRIMINALS

In 1945, after the war ended, a special court was created to bring to trial the top Nazi officials responsible for the Holocaust. The International Military Tribunal at Nuremberg convened in November, and the trials continued until 1 October 1946. The court indicted 24 people and 6 Nazi organizations, including the Gestapo. During the trials much of the evidence about the planning of Kristallnacht became

Military police kept a close eye on Nazi officials during war crimes trials in Nuremberg.

public. Twelve of the defendants at Nuremberg were condemned to death, including Hermann Göring. He killed himself with a cyanide pill on 15 October 1946, the day before he was scheduled to be hanged.

And what became of Herschel Grynszpan? He was never tried for his crime. The French government was afraid to stage a trial. If a jury found Grynszpan not guilty, the Nazis would retaliate against France. When Germany invaded France, Grynszpan was transferred to the Sachsenhausen concentration camp. The Nazis intended to use Grynszpan's trial as a propaganda tool, so he received good care in prison. They were never able to make the trial happen on their terms, though. Grynszpan spent most of the war at Sachsenhausen. But by 1942 his name disappeared from German record books. No one knows for sure what happened to him, but it's widely believed that he died in the camp.

His family, for the most part, was much more fortunate. His parents and siblings were able to escape Poland during the German invasion. They settled in the Soviet Union and moved to Israel after the war. His uncle Abraham, however, died in Auschwitz.

TIMELINE

11 November 1918
World War I
officially ends

13 March 1938
Anschluss, the
annexation of
Austria, occurs

8-9 November 1923
Adolf Hitler leads a
failed Nazi attempt,
known as the Beer Hall
Putsch, to take over the
German government

26 April 1938
New rule requires
declaration of all Jewish
property valued at more
than 5,000 reichsmarks

9 June 1938
Main synagogue in
Munich is torn down
and a car park is built
in its place

15 September 1935
Nuremberg Laws
are enacted

6-15 July 1938
International conference
to discuss the issue of
Jewish refugees takes
place in Evian, France

17 August 1938

Decree is issued requiring Jews to add the names Israel and Sarah

5 October 1938

Jewish passports are no longer valid; identity cards are required

28 October 1938

12,000 Jews of Polish origin are expelled to Zbaszyn near the Polish border

7 November 1938

Herschel Grynszpan shoots Ernst vom Rath in Paris

9 November 1938

Vom Rath dies; Joseph Goebbels gives a speech during a Nazi gathering and blames all Jews for vom Rath's death

9–10 November 1938

Jewish businesses, homes and synagogues are attacked during Kristallnacht

11 November 1938

Goebbels holds a press conference for foreign correspondents and blames German citizens for Kristallnacht

▶ **12 November 1938**
Decree is issued demanding "atonement payments" from German Jews for Kristallnacht damages

▶ **3 December 1938**
The Decree on the Utilization of Jewish Property forces Jewish business owners to sell their property to non-Jews; they receive a fraction of the property's value

▶ **14 November 1938**
Jews are forbidden to attend cultural events

▶ **6 December 1938**
Jews are forbidden to drive or walk in certain places

▶ **15 November 1938**
Jewish children are banned from German schools; US President Franklin D. Roosevelt publicly condemns the Nazi actions during Kristallnacht

▶ **1 September 1939**
Germany invades Poland; two days later, Britain and France declare war on Germany; World War II begins

▶ **July 1944**
Soviet soldiers liberate
the death camp
Majdanek in Poland

▶ **30 April 1945**
Hitler commits suicide
in his bunker; Joseph
Goebbels commits
suicide the next day

▶ **8 May 1945**
Germany surrenders to
the Allies; the war ends
in Europe

▶ **14 August 1945**
Japan's Emperor
Hirohito agrees to
surrender to the Allies;
the war officially ends in
September

GLOSSARY

allies friends or helpers; when capitalized, refers to Britain and its allies during major wars

anti-Semitism prejudice or discrimination against Jewish people

Aryan term used by Nazis to describe a supposed master race of pure-blooded Germans with blonde hair and blue eyes

assassination murder of someone who is well known or important, often for political reasons

bar mitzvah ceremony and celebration that takes place on or near a Jewish boy's 13th birthday; girls have a similar ceremony called a bat mitzvah

chancellor the head of government in some countries such as Germany

communism system in which goods and property are owned by the government and shared in common; communist rulers limit personal freedoms to achieve their goals

concentration camps prison camps where thousands of inmates are held under harsh conditions

constitution system of laws that state the rights of the people and the powers of the government

coup sudden change of government, often by force

democracy form of government in which the people elect their leaders

dictator ruler who takes complete control of a country, often unjustly

discrimination unfair treatment of a person or group, often because of race, religion, gender, sexual preference or age

emigrate leave a home country to settle in another country permanently

fascism government system that promotes extreme nationalism, repression and anti-communism, and is ruled by a dictator

führer German word meaning "leader"

incumbent the current holder of an office

indict charge with a crime

inflation increase in prices

kosher prepared according to Jewish dietary laws

orator someone who is skilled at public speaking

paranoia irrational or unfounded feelings of mistrust and suspicion

parliament group of people elected to make laws

pogrom organized attack on a minority group, especially Jews

putsch violent attempt to overthrow a government

reparations payments made to make amends for wrongdoing

swastika cross with bent arms that the Nazi Party used as its symbol

synagogue Jewish place of worship

FIND OUT MORE

BOOKS

Hitler and Kristallnacht (Days of Decision),
Andrew Langley (Raintree, 2014)

Saving the Persecuted (Heroes of World War II),
Brian and Brenda Williams (Raintree, 2015)

Survivors of the Holocaust, Kath Shackleton
(Franklin Watts, 2016)

The Usborne Introduction to The Second World War,
Paul Dowswell (Usborne Publishing Ltd, 2005)

WEBSITES

**www.bbc.co.uk/bitesize/ks3/history/20th_century/
holocaust/revision/2/**
Learn more about the Holocaust.

www.bbc.co.uk/programmes/p0274903
Follow the story of Ruth and her family as they flee
Nazi Germany.

www.iwm.org.uk/history/second-world-war
Discover articles and artefacts related to World War II from the
Imperial War Museum archives, from everyday life during the
war to the role of government propaganda.

COMPREHENSION QUESTIONS

Germany's leaders felt that the rest of the world had treated the country unfairly after World War I. Do you think this treatment justified their actions after the war? Why or why not? Support your answer with evidence from the text.

Most non-Jewish people in Germany and Austria didn't try to help their Jewish neighbours during Kristallnacht for fear that they would also be punished. What do you think about their lack of action? Would you have done things differently in the same situation?

Before and during World War II, Jewish people were discriminated against by various governments. Why do you think people today still face discrimination because of race, religion or other factors?

SOURCE NOTES

Page 7, line 10: Mitchell G. Bard. *48 Hours of Kristallnacht Night of Destruction/Dawn of the Holocaust: An Oral History*. Guilford, Conn.: Lyons Press, 2008, pp. 60–61.

Page 10, line 9: Ibid., p. 62.

Page 11, line 2: "German mobs' vengeance on Jews—Nov. 11, 1938." *The Telegraph*. 11 Nov. 2008. 21 Dec. 2016. http://www.telegraph.co.uk/history/britain-at-war/3418286/German-mobs-vengeance-on-Jews-Nov-11-1938.html

Page 19, line 5: "The German Hyperinflation, 1923." Commanding Heights: The Battle for the World Economy. PBS. 21 Dec. 2016. https://www.pbs.org/wgbh/commandingheights/shared/minitext/ess_germanhyperinflation.html

Page 31, col. 2, line 1: Marion A. Kaplan. *Between Dignity and Despair: Jewish Life in Nazi Germany*. New York: Oxford University Press, 1998, pp. 33–34.

Page 36, col. 2, line 2: "The Rise of Adolf Hitler." The History Place. 27 Dec. 2016. http://www.historyplace.com/worldwar2/riseofhitler/father.htm

Page 43, col. 2, line 2: *Between Dignity and Despair: Jewish Life in Nazi Germany*, p. 35.

Page 44, line 3: Anthony Read and David Fisher. *Kristallnacht: The Nazi Night of Terror*. New York: Times Books, 1989, p. 28.

Page 51, col. 2, line 2: "Chronology of Jewish Persecution: 1933." Jewish Virtual Library. 27 Dec. 2016. http://www.jewishvirtuallibrary.org/timeline-of-jewish-persecution-in-the-holocaust

Page 53, line 5: *Kristallnacht: The Nazi Night of Terror*, p. 30.

Page 58, line 18: Jonathan Kirsch. *The Short, Strange Life of Herschel Grynszpan: A Boy Avenger, a Nazi Diplomat, and a Murder in Paris*. New York: Liveright Publishing Corporation, 2013, p. 83.

Page 60, line 16: *Kristallnacht: The Nazi Night of Terror*, p. 48.

Page 62, line 8: Ibid., p. 51.

Page 64, line 1: *The Short, Strange Life of Herschel Grynszpan: A Boy Avenger, a Nazi Diplomat, and a Murder in Paris,* pp. 108–109

Page 64, line 16: *Kristallnacht: The Nazi Night of Terror,* p. 8.

Page 65, col. 1, line 8: Ibid., p. 51.

Page 68, line 5: Ibid., p. 61.

Page 68, line 21: Volker Ullrich. *Hitler: Ascent, 1889–1939.* New York: Alfred A. Knopf, 2016, p. 669.

Page 69, line 9: *Kristallnacht: The Nazi Night of Terror,* p. 62.

Page 69, line 18: Anthony Read. *The Devil's Disciples: Hitler's Inner Circle.* New York: W. W. Norton, 2004, p. 510.

Page 75, col. 1, line 10: Rabbi Marvin Hier. "Kristallnacht Seventy Years Later—'Was There No Space in the World for Us?'" 2008. 28 Dec. 2016. Simon Wiesenthal Center. http://www.wiesenthal.com/site/ apps/nlnet/content2.aspx?c=lsKWLbPJLnF&b=4924937&ct=6346483

Page 77, line 1: Lyn Smith. *Remembering: Voices of the Holocaust: A New History in the Words of the Men and Women Who Survived.* New York: Carroll & Graf, 2006, p. 50.

Page 77, line 20: Martin Gilbert. *Kristallnacht: Prelude to Destruction.* New York: HarperCollins, 2006, pp. 80–81.

Page 82, col. 1, line 9: *Kristallnacht: The Nazi Night of Terror,* p. 166.

Page 86, line 4: Ibid., p. 162.

Page 88, line 2: Rafael Medoff. "Kristallnacht—and the World's Response." November 2003. 28 Dec. 2016. The David S. Wyman Institute for Holocaust Studies. http://www.wymaninstitute.org/ articles/2003-11-kristalln.php

Page 88, line 6: Arthur Sears Henning. "President Rips into Nazis for Harassing Jews." *The Daily Chicago Tribune.* 16 Nov. 1938, p. 3. 28 Dec. 2016. http://archives.chicagotribune.com/1938/11/16/page/3/article/ president-rips-into-nazis-for-harassing-jews

SELECT BIBLIOGRAPHY

"Adolf Hitler." History. 29 Dec. 2016. http://www.history.com/topics/world-war-ii/adolf-hitler

Bard, Mitchell G. *48 Hours of Kristallnacht Night of Destruction/Dawn of the Holocaust: An Oral History.* Guilford, Conn.: Lyons Press, 2008.

"Commanding Heights: The Battle for the World Economy." 21 April 2017. PBS. http://www.pbs.org/wgbh/commandingheights/

Gilbert, Martin. *Kristallnacht: Prelude to Destruction.* New York: HarperCollins, 2006.

Henning, Arthur Sears. "President Rips into Nazis for Harassing Jews." *The Daily Chicago Tribune.* 16 Nov. 1938, p. 3. 28 Dec. 2016. http://archives.chicagotribune.com/1938/11/16/page/3/article/president-rips-into-nazis-for-harassing-jews

Hier, Marvin. "Kristallnacht Seventy Years Later—'Was There No Space in the World for Us?'" 2008. 28 Dec. 2016. Simon Wiesenthal Center. http://www.wiesenthal.com/site/apps/nlnet/content2.aspx?c=lsKWLbPJLnF&b=4924937&ct=6346483

Holocaust Education & Archive Research Team. 29 Dec. 2016. http://www.holocaustresearchproject.org/toc.html

Jewish Virtual Library. 29 Dec. 2016. http://www.jewishvirtuallibrary.org

Kaplan, Marion A. *Between Dignity and Despair: Jewish Life in Nazi Germany.* New York: Oxford University Press, 1998.

Kirsch, Jonathan. *The Short, Strange Life of Herschel Grynszpan: A Boy Avenger, a Nazi Diplomat, and a Murder in Paris.* New York: Liveright Publishing Corporation, 2013.

Laqueur, Walter. *Generation Exodus: The Fate of Young Jewish Refugees from Nazi Germany.* Hanover, N.H.: Brandeis University Press, 2001.

Medoff, Rafael. "Kristallnacht—and the World's Response." November 2003. 28 Dec. 2016. The David S. Wyman Institute for Holocaust Studies. http://www.wymaninstitute.org/articles/2003-11-kristalln.php

Read, Anthony. *The Devil's Disciples: Hitler's Inner Circle.* New York: W. W. Norton, 2004.

Read, Anthony, and David Fisher. *Kristallnacht: The Nazi Night of Terror.* New York: Times Books, 1989.

"The Rise of Adolf Hitler." The History Place. 29 Dec. 2016. http://www.historyplace.com/worldwar2/riseofhitler/index.htm

Schwab, Gerald. *The Day the Holocaust Began: The Odyssey of Herschel Grynszpan.* New York: Praeger, 1990.

Smith, Lyn. *Remembering: Voices of the Holocaust: A New History in the Words of the Men and Women Who Survived.* New York: Carroll & Graf, 2006.

Ullrich, Volker. *Hitler: Ascent, 1889–1939.* New York: Alfred A. Knopf, 2016.

United States Holocaust Memorial Museum. 29 Dec. 2016. https://www.ushmm.org

INDEX